Happy Birthday to <u>SKYLER</u> on
her 6th Birthday

Much Love, hugs and Kisses
Mary Frances

Susan Titus Osborn & Christine Harder Tangvald

Ten Friends Together

Pictures by Becky Radtke

CPH
SAINT LOUIS

The fair's today—downtown—it's true.
The fair's today—with lots to do!
I will sit right over there ...

ONE friend ...
going to the fair.

You can sit right over there ...
THREE friends ... going to the fair!

Rachel, Rachel, it's so true ...
We're so glad you're coming too!
You can sit right over there ...

EIGHT friends ... going to the fair.

You can sit right over there ...
TEN friends ... going to the fair!

for He is good (Psalm 107:1).

Thank You for our friends who share.
One to ten—we all had fun.
Thank You, Jesus, GOD'S OWN SON!

Hi Kids!

Did you know that God made you special? He made every one of your friends special too. He loves each of you very much. He made you unique. That means that you are so special that no one else is exactly like you. God loves you so much that He takes special care of you every day. He takes special care of your friends too.

And God did something even more wonderful. He sent His Son, Jesus, to be your friend and Savior. Jesus died and rose again so that all your sins could be forgiven. That way, you and your friends can live in heaven with Jesus forever. Isn't that super? That's why these nine friends are coming to the missions fair. They want to tell others the Good News about their best friend, Jesus. They want you to join them. Whom can you tell about Jesus?

Love,
Susan and Christine